THE G.I. SERIES

THE ILLUSTRATED HISTORY OF THE AMERICAN SOLDIER, HIS UNIFORM AND HIS EQUIPMENT

Bluecoats
The U.S. Army in the West
1848–1897

John P. Langellier

Greenhill Books
LONDON

Stackpole Books
PENNSYLVANIA

Greenhill Books

Bluecoats: The U.S. Army in the West, 1848–1897 first published 1995 by Greenhill Books, Lionel Leventhal Limited, Park House, 1 Russell Gardens, London NW11 9NN
and
Stackpole Books, 5067 Ritter Road, Mechanicsburg, PA 17055, USA.

British Library Cataloguing in Publication Data
Langellier, John P.
Bluecoats: The US Army in the West, 1848–1897. – (G.I.: The Illustrated History of the American Soldier, His Uniform & His Equipment; Vol.2)
I. Title II. Series
355.80973
ISBN 1-85367-221-1

Library of Congress Cataloging-in-Publication Data
Langellier, H. Phillip
Bluecoats: The US Army in the West, 1848–1897 / by John P. Langellier.
80p. 26cm. – (G.I. ; 2)
ISBN 1-85367-221-1 (pb)
1. United States. Army–Uniforms–History–19th century. 2. United States. Army–Equipment–History–19th century. 3. West (U.S.)–History–1848–1860. 4. West (U.S.)–History–1860–1890.
I. Title II. Series: G.I. (Series) (London, England) ; 2.
UC483.L35 1995
355.3'1'097309034–dc20

Designed and edited by DAG Publications Ltd
Designed by David Gibbons.
Layout by Anthony A. Evans.
Printed in Hong Kong.

ACKNOWLEDGEMENTS

In addition to the various institutions and individuals who have provided images for this publication the author wishes to thank Michael Duchemin, Kevin Mulroy and James Nottage, all colleagues from the Autry Museum of Western Heritage, for their special assistance. Also, the photographic work of Susan Einstein is most appreciated. Finally, this work is dedicated to my colleague Gordon S. Chappell.

ABBREVIATIONS

AMWH	Autry Museum of Western Heritage
BL	Bancroft Library, Berkeley, CA
FAM	Frontier Army Museum, Ft. Leavenworth, KS
FDNHS	Fort Davis National Historic Site
FLNHS	Fort Laramie National Historic Site
LBNB	Little Bighorn National Battlefield
LC	Library of Congress
NARS	National Archives Records Service
KSHS	Kansas State Historical Society, Topeka
RBM	Reno Battlefield Museum, Garryowen, MT
SI	Smithsonian Institution, Museum of American History
USAMHI	US Army Military History Institute, Carlisle Barracks, PA
UKL	Pennell Collection, Kansas Collections, University of Kansas Libraries, Lawrence
USCM	US Cavalry Museum, Fort Riley, KS
WSM	Wyoming State Museum, Cheyenne

THE G.I. SERIES

Bluecoats
The U.S. Army in the West
1848–1897

In 1846 Cave Johnson Couts, a second lieutenant in the First Regiment of US Dragoons, rode to California where he and his comrades would participate in the war against Mexico. He appears in the single-breasted dark blue wool frock coat authorized for company grade officers. The buttons are gilt with a spread eagle motif that has a 'd' (dragoons) in the center. The special shoulder-straps he is wearing are unique to that branch and were adopted in 1839, as was the forage cap which tops off his field uniform. This basic outfit remained regulation for company grade officers into 1852. (Huntington Library)

BLUECOATS
THE US ARMY IN THE WEST,
1848–1897

Early in the history of the United States its army was called upon to serve as the vanguard of western expansion. Soldiers fought Indians living east of the Mississippi River so that settlements could be established in former American Indian domains. Later, these same forces were given the responsibility of keeping whites away from lands known as reservations which were set aside for the exclusive use of Indians. Military parties also set out to explore and chart unknown territories beginning with the bold ventures of Meriwether Lewis and William Clark, two infantry officers assigned to probe the vast Louisiana Purchase. In the years to come, more martial expeditions would set out for the frontier under military men such as Zebulon Pike, John Charles Frémont, and many others who often proved intrepid explorers and able map makers. In their wake, new army forts were built throughout the 1800s to keep pace with the westward movement that was gathering strength with each succeeding generation.

But the U.S. Army's presence would not be felt in strength so far as the West was concerned until forts began to be built beyond the Mississippi. Even then, it was the war between the United States and Mexico that prompted the deployment of more troops to the region. In 1848, at the conclusion of that conflict, extensive territory was added to the U.S.A. by conquest, treaty and purchase.

Thereafter, troops would be posted in Texas, New Mexico, California, and elsewhere in the newly acquired lands as the tide of westward expansion heightened. For most of the period from the late 1840s into the end of the 1850s frontier troops garrisoned scattered posts from the Mississippi to the Pacific and from the borders with Mexico to the south and Canada to the

north. Then, in 1861, things changed when the civil war that erupted between northern and southern sections of the nation eventually spilled westward. Regular Army forces withdrew from most of the West but would be replaced by volunteer units formed in the various Western states and territories. After four years of fighting between the Union and Confederacy, the volunteers ended their service and the U.S. Army again turned most of its attention to the West where white migration was heightening. This increased contact and its resultant friction between Indians and non-Indians came at a time when the army was being reduced to a skeleton force compared to the strength it had gained in the war, when the Yankees had fielded upwards of a million men against the South. By 1866, that strength had plummeted to an authorized 54,000 troops, but in reality only about two-thirds of that number were ever raised.

Ultimately, only twenty-five regiments of infantry and ten of cavalry (including four units of African American enlisted men) were available for duty at the far-flung, usually small, outposts from the Canadian border to Mexico and from the Mississippi to the Pacific Ocean. Only a few thousand combat troops were called upon to carry out the federal government's orders in an area that comprised more than half of the continental U.S.A. These frontier regulars policed the plains, patrolled the borders and brought order to the deserts and mountains, much as they had done prior to the war. They chased bandits, revolutionaries, and, on many occasions, pursued illusive and formidable Indians including the Apache, Cheyenne, Comanche, Kiowa, Modoc, Nez Perce, Sioux, and others who fought valiantly to retain their old way of life in the face of overwhelming odds as the tide of white expansion encroached upon their hunting grounds. To complicate matters, Congress allotted the barest budget to sustain the army, and on two occasions failed to pass appropriations to pay the troops. This caused considerable hardship for many months until their pay was reinstated.

Geography also presented challenges. Regional departments were formed and each area was guarded jealously by the commander in charge. Because Indians did not always stay within the boundaries of one command, pursuit by troops from one region into another presented yet another source of bickering and occasionally inhibited their effectiveness.

Despite such internal bickering the troops managed to carry out their diverse missions. Although called upon to take the field with astonishing regularity, most of their time was spent in the forts. These were usually little more than a collection of buildings around a central rectangle – the parade ground – the heart of the military community; normally flanked by the officers' quarters on one side and the enlisted barracks on the other. Here stood the flagstaff with the Stars and Stripes, the symbol of government authority. Here the men assembled and carried out the rituals of their trade – guard mounting, reviews and other ceremonies. Here or nearby the men cleaned their equipment, drilled, built quarters, tended livestock, and even grew vegetables.

This last activity served to supplement the prescribed ration which tended to be monotonous and was far from constituting a balanced diet. Meat, either beef or pork, was a staple, with rice or potatoes, bread (baked daily by troops detailed to the post bakery), beans (by the 1880s), making up the basic fare, all being washed down by strong coffee. One diary account of the times wryly recorded the lack of variety when the writer stated: 'We have a change of diet: hardtack [a thick cracker], bacon and coffee for breakfast; raw bacon and [hard] tack for dinner; fried bacon and hard bread for supper.'

Fortunately, men and officers alike could add to the larder by fishing or hunting. Depending on the location of the fort, trout or other fish could be caught, and the pursuit of deer, elk, pronghorn antelope, prairie hen, duck, grouse, and rabbit, as well as wild pigs, turkeys, and geese supplemented the ration and proved a pleasant recreation. Hunting bison provided a further diversion and a change of diet.

As indicated previously, fresh vegetables were grown by the troops or purchased from the local commissary or the post trader, both of which facilities offered goods that the government did not provide. On holidays and other occasions, the troops also pooled the money from their company funds which they, not the army, had contributed, and purchased, for example, tomatoes, mushrooms, oysters, and lobster, all canned and shipped from the eastern United States or even Europe, together with canned or fresh fruit, eggs, turkey, ham, or other commodities considered to be delicacies. The post trader, later known as the post exchange, carried other things too: clothing, dry goods, cigars, tobacco, beer, and wine.

Restricting the types and quantity of alcohol available at the trader was of concern to many commanders as a means of maintaining a degree of moderation in the consumption of liquor. The frontier military had its share of those who drank to excess. When they were unable to buy their spirits on post, all too often nearby towns or other sources could be counted upon to supply not only strong drink but also places for gambling and prostitution. Some of these off post operations, which were nicknamed 'hog ranches', became a serious challenge to the maintenance of discipline. Men would get drunk, catch venereal diseases, gamble away their pay, and brawl – with consequences ranging from minor injuries to death.

An officer from the garrison was given the dubious honor of rounding up the rowdies. On such an assignment a bystander recalled, 'one of the men, full or liquor and beer, grabbed the officer of the day, took his belt off, and threw him under a billiard table'. A guard detail subdued the intoxicated offender. Such clashes regularly filled the cells of the local stockade.

In many instances, soldiers failed to return from their sprees. Men decided to desert while away from the fort or even when they were in garrison. In fact, desertion rates ran extremely high in many years, at least among the regiments of white enlisted personnel. Conversely, the regiments of black troops tended to have far fewer instances of desertion and the men in these units more regularly re-enlisted. Apparently many African Americans looked upon military service as a profession bringing pride and stature rather than as a temporary job to be abandoned at will.

Certain commanders tried to deal with the problems that led to desertion, including the abuse of liquor, by offering wholesome alternative outlets for soldiers' free time. Sports provided one means of enhancing morale and maintaining physical fitness. Baseball was an early transplant to forts in the West. Track and field events together with shooting competitions were common, and lawn tennis, gymnastics and bowling, in a few instances, provided diversions. The men of Fort Grant, Arizona Territory, even dug a small pond at their desert outpost where they could paddle about in a tiny rowboat! More commonly, natural lakes and rivers near a garrison provided fine sites for picnics and swimming; in winter in colder climates, ice-skating, slides and sleigh-rides.

Warm weather brought drives in carriages, at least for officers, and horseback rides or frontier versions of fox hunts, the prey usually being coyotes. When women took part, side-saddles were required. Even peddling one of the varieties of bicycles which became popular in the Victorian era might be attempted. Moreover, horse races caused a break in routine and some posts, such as Fort Leavenworth, Kansas, had their own tracks.

Men played cards, billiards, or checkers, in barracks, or at the trader's store where they could have a sandwich while reading newspapers, or reading and writing letters. Rudimentary post libraries carried newspapers, periodicals, and some popular books, including foreign language publications because so many of the enlisted men had come from Germany and other European countries. In fact, upwards of 30 per cent of the privates and non-commissioned officers were born abroad, most of this group coming from Ireland, England, Scotland, Germany, Canada, France, and Italy. The remainder of the rank and file were born in the United States, including by the 1890s a small number of American Indians who had enlisted. Previously, Indians of various tribes had been employed as scouts.

Some men born in the U.S.A. and not a few of the immigrants brought musical traditions and talents with them. Guitars, banjos, fiddles, and other instruments were played for personal pleasure or to entertain the garrison. Impromptu orchestras might be formed, and at certain larger garrisons regimental bands often were on hand to liven up social gatherings and to add pomp and circumstance at martial formations. Ultimately, these bands constituted a vital part of the garrison life at those forts which were fortunate enough to enjoy their services. They helped pass idle hours for those in uniform as well as their families and local civilians. In this regard, the military music makers helped to strengthen goodwill between the army and its non-military neighbors. Moreover, the bands boosted morale and introduced some people to a variety of music which they might not have been familiar with previously, ranging from strictly martial airs to classical symphonies and popular tunes of the time.

Bands held concerts and played at dances known to the Victorian-era soldiers as 'hops'. They likewise performed in some instances for theatricals. Amateur stage companies came into being at some posts, such as Fort Leavenworth which took considerable pride in its troupe who regularly took to the stage with everything from melodramas to Gilbert and Sullivan's 'Pirates of Penzance'. Touring companies also were welcome at posts or their nearby civilian communities, as were infrequent novelties such as circuses and steam calliopes.

All this is not to say that the lot of the officer and his family or that of his subordinates was just one diversion after another. In fact, the routine of a garrison was anything but exciting. Cleaning stables was dirty work and seemed somewhat absurd when one considers that the outfit issued by the army for this filthy job consisted of a white linen coat and matching trousers. Chopping wood, construction details, and all manner of other chores had to be dealt with, alongside military functions from practice with saber, bayonet, and firearms, to marching for foot soldiers and equitation training for cavalrymen, based largely upon the complex procedures set forth in manuals written by Civil War General Emory Upton, one of the U.S. Army's most influential tacticians and strategists of the late 1800s.

So regimented was this life that Lieutenant Colonel George Custer's spouse, who was a capable author (Elizabeth Bacon Custer), noted that the bugle served as an hourly monitor. 'It told us when to eat, to sleep, to march, and to go to church. Its clear tones reminded us, should there be any physical ailments, that we must go to the doctor, and if the lazy soldier was disposed to lounge about the company's barracks, or his indolent officer to loll his life away in a hammock on the gallery of his quarters, the bugle's sharp call summoned him to "drill" or "dress parade".'

In the latter case, cavalry troopers regularly fell in for formations on the parade ground in their finery. In the 1860s this consisted of a short blue jacket with yellow braid topped by a black hat which looped up on the right side very much like something out of *The Three Musketeers*. Beginning in the early 1870s, the horse soldiers switched to a helmet with yellow horsetail plume, a piece of headgear which took its inspiration from European models of the time. Infantrymen had the same black hat with a long frock coat trimmed in blue during the 1860s, then adopted stiff caps with a pompon, before changing over to their own dress helmet which was topped off with a brass spike as of 1881.

More functional uniforms were prescribed for other garrison wear and field use. Typically, on less formal occasions, troops had a loose fitting blue blouse which from 1872 to 1884 was trimmed with piping to indicate the branch of service, yellow designating cavalry, light blue for infantry, and so forth. Forage caps after the French fashion were regulation, but broad-brimmed hats similar to those adopted by cowboys in the West were favored on campaign. Black versions were issued throughout the 1880s, although a brownish-grey version began to be available from the early 1880s. Light blue wool trousers were also part of the basic outfit.

Various cartridge carrying devices were used; leather ammunition boxes and pouches were standard during the early years after the Civil War, but these were phased out in favour of belts with cartridge loops by the 1870s, at least for field service.

Weapons included sabers and bayonets, though these two items were used more for garrison duty than for combat. Conversely, rifles and carbines were the mainstay of infantry and cavalry troops respectively. In the former instance, single-shot muzzle loading rifles were sent West at first, but metallic cartridge breechloaders soon replaced the older models.

Cavalrymen had extra fire power because they were issued with revolvers. While weapons improved, marksmanship was indifferent during the 1860s through the 1870s when the troops began to require target practice not long after Custer's command went down in a resounding defeat at the Little Big Horn.

In the long run, victories were more frequent than defeats. Superior numbers and technology, together with numerous other factors eventually led to the success of the military in pacifying the West. Through it all life was difficult for the soldiers and their families. Braving blizzards, bullets, boredom, and other hardships, the U.S. Army in the West compiled an impressive record. The hard-riding troopers and the diligent foot soldiers in their hot blue wool uniforms left a lasting mark on the region which still can be seen today at many historic sites, and which can be retraced in the writings and photographs from this bygone era.

FOR FURTHER READING

Josephy, Alvin M., Jr. *The Civil War in the American West.* New York: Alfred A. Knopf, 1991.

McChristian, Douglas C. *The U.S. Army in the West: Uniforms, Equipment and Weapons, 1870-1880.* Norman: University of Oklahoma Press, 1995.

Utley, Robert M. *Frontier Regulars: The United States Army and the Indian, 1866-1891.* New York: Macmillan, 1973.

— *Frontiersmen in Blue: The United States Army and the Indian, 1845-1865.* New York: Macmillan, 1967.

Above: In 1854 a jacket similar to that worn before 1851 for all troops was again prescribed for mounted soldiers, including light artillery and mounted rifles personnel (exemplified here by the figure in the background, far right), with green for mounted rifles and scarlet for light artillery. A cap with a pompon and welt of the same color cloth was combined with this outfit which supposedly was to serve for all garrison functions and field service, as was the *chasseurs-à-pied* 1855-pattern single-breasted frock coat with its full pleated waist that was worn by foot troops such as the heavy artillery private in the background to the left and the heavy artillery private in the center foreground (with scarlet trim) speaking to an infantry first sergeant (with sky-blue facings). As of 1854, brass shoulder-scales and collar numerals were to be worn by all troops, mounted or dismounted, and collar numerals supposedly were worn to designate regimental affiliation for all troops through 1857. Although the artist Henry Ogden, who rendered this illustration for the quartermaster department in the 1880s, depicts welts with branch colors on the outside seams of the trousers, this trim was eliminated by General Orders No. 1, 20 January 1854. (AMWH)

Above: The pattern of uniform adopted for dress in 1872 included a cap for enlisted foot troops with pompon (white for infantry, scarlet for artillery, and so forth) and a helmet for enlisted cavalry, light artillery, and signal service personnel (with yellow trim for cavalry as seen here in the case of a sergeant). The officers' cap was surmounted by white or scarlet cock feathers respectively for infantry and heavy artillery, and light artillery officers together with cavalry officers followed the lead of enlisted men in terms of scarlet or yellow plumes respectively. Facings on the dress coats issued to other ranks included yellow for cavalry, scarlet for artillery, and medium blue for infantry. (AMWH)

Below: Left to right: field grade officer of artillery with scarlet buffalo hair plume; company grade officer of heavy artillery; captain of cavalry; second lieutenant of signal corps with dark blue trousers and no trouser stripes, as followed the same style for staff officers and generals, all in full dress of the 1881 pattern. (Kurt Cox Collection)

Left: Left to right: sergeant major of cavalry; private of cavalry; sergeant of infantry; private of infantry, all in the regulation dress uniform of the 1881–4 period. (Kurt Cox Collection)

Below left: Left to right: sergeant of signal service and private of signal service in 1881-pattern dress uniform; private of artillery in 1874-pattern blouse and 1880-pattern summer helmet; cavalry and light artillery stable-frock and overalls with the 1876-pattern black campaign hat. (Kurt Cox Collection)

Below: Left to right: private of infantry in the 1884–1903-pattern dress uniform; infantry officer indicated by 1½-inch white leg stripes and white-backed shoulder-straps as of 1884, with the 1880-pattern summer helmet having chin-chain and spike attached for garrison wear; private of either the Twenty-fourth or Twenty-fifth Infantry Regiment in marching order with 1872-pattern forage cap in lieu of the more popular campaign hat; infantry sergeant major in garrison with white facings adopted in 1884 and white enlisted man's model of the 1880-pattern summer helmet; sergeant of light artillery in garrison indicated by scarlet facings and the model 1840 light artillery saber; cavalry trooper in stable uniform with the drab campaign hat; Indian scout in field kit with the drab campaign hat. A special black campaign hat with low round crown was adopted in 1890 for Indian scouts and issued in small quantities. (LC)

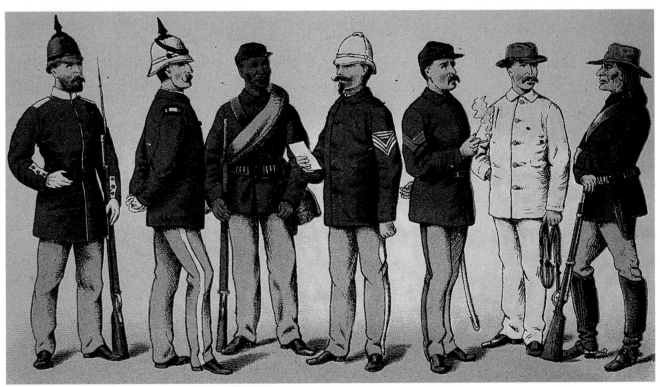

Above: Left to right: Company musician heavy artillery, signal sergeant, post ordnance sergeant, post commissary sergeant, hospital steward, and post quartermaster sergeant all in the 1885-pattern full dress uniform. The hospital steward, however, is wearing the gold lace dress chevrons which would be adopted in 1887. (AMWH)

Above: A general officer, indicated by the type of galloons on his overcoat, the black velvet band on his forage cap, and the dark blue trousers without stripe, is depicted beside a lieutenant colonel of artillery and a captain of cavalry, all of whom wear the officers' 1884-pattern overcoat. To their right stands a corporal of cavalry in the enlisted overcoat of either the 1885 or 1886 pattern. (AMWH)

Above: Left to right: In background mounted cavalry troop bugler in the 1887-pattern dress coat (indicated by the darker shade of yellow than the previous 1885-pattern cavalry dress coat); infantry corporal in the 1884-pattern dress uniform facings, a cavalry private and a cavalry sergeant, both in the 1887-pattern dress cavalry uniform. In the background to the right is a private of infantry and a company musician of infantry in their 1884-pattern dress uniforms. The musician has a double pair of ½-inch white stripes on his trousers, a practice which had been customary at some posts, for musicians' prior to 1881, although this was not approved officially until a general order of 1883. (AMWH)

Above: Captain Henry Little of the Seventh U.S. Infantry sat for this portrait in his dress coatee of the pattern adopted in 1832 and which remained regulation through 1852. The epaulets, buttons, and lace on the collar and cuffs are silver bullion. The belt is white buff leather with an interlocking buckle. (USAMHI)

Left: An unknown infantry field grade officer (probably a lieutenant colonel) wears the dark blue center shoulder-straps with silver border prescribed for infantry officers through 1852. The bugle device is the silver embroidered insignia which was sewn to the lower end of the rear tails of dress coatees such as that worn by Captain Little. This addition, although non regulation, seems to have been fairly common judging from photographs of the pre-war era. J. Craig Nannos Collection

Right: Orlando Poe became a second lieutenant of Topographical Engineers on 7 October 1856. He wears the garrison uniform which doubled for field use typical of company grade officers of the 1850s. He also retains the old 1839-pattern forage cap rather than appearing with the 1851-pattern cap with pompon that was called for in regulations. (USAMHI)

Above: A youthful infantry officer and his lady pose for a portrait in about 1852. He is in the new regulation company grade uniform prescribed the year before, including the tall cap with removable sky-blue pompon and embroidered hunting horn device, the insignia for infantry officers. He has chosen to wear the shoulder-straps, prescribed for field and general garrison wear, over his epaulets which was not a common practice. The size of the fringe of the epaulets indicates that he is a subaltern. The fact that these devices and his shoulder-straps are plain marks him as a second lieutenant. (USAMHI)

Right: In the late 1850s Second Lieutenant Kirby Smith of the élite Topographical Engineers (later to become a general officer in the Confederate Army) went to Utah with a major surveying expedition. An embroidered wreath with shield in the center on the front of the new forage cap indicates his branch. This item of head-dress was unique to engineers from 1857 through 1858 when the Secretary of War ordered that it be adopted for all branches and ranks. The transition was gradual, but by the time of the Civil War this cap was typical. (NARS)

Right: Surgeon Albert Myer, serving in Texas in the mid-1850s, has put aside almost all indications that he is a U.S. Army officer save for his 1851-pattern eagle belt plate and some of his accoutrements. Adopting civilian clothing, accessories, and equipment was a frequent response when government issue items did not meet local environmental conditions. (NARS)

Left: In this 1858 image of Lieutenant Smith taking solar readings at Camp Floyd, Utah Territory, the young topographical engineer wears a short-style jacket usually prescribed for officers serving with mounted forces. (LC)

Above: In 1858 a new hat, which took its inspiration from a pattern issued to the First and Second Cavalry Regiments from three years earlier, was prescribed for all troops. This fur felt headpiece looped on the left side for foot soldiers and on the right side for mounted troops. Company letters and the regimental number were affixed to the front of the crown. A black ostrich feather and worsted cords ending in tassels were also prescribed, as was a sheet brass eagle device which was used to hold the turned up side in place. For dismounted men a single-breasted frock coat with nine buttons down the front was to be worn with the hat for formal occasions. Trim was yellow for engineers, scarlet for heavy artillery, crimson for ordnance and hospital stewards, and sky-blue for infantry. In addition, a special lace design ornamented the front of a musician's coat as seen in this case for an infantry bugler. Dark blue trousers were regulation from 1858 through 1861 and from that year through 1872 sky-blue trousers were worn with this uniform. (SI)

Right: Heavy artillery units, such as these men mounting guard at the fortifications on Alcatraz Island in San Francisco Bay, also wore the frock coat, brass shoulder-scales, and dress hat for parades, inspections, and the like. The front of the coat was plain for all save musicians. A lieutenant or captain stands in the front center with his crimson silk sash worn over the right shoulder and down to the left hip, thus indicating that he is serving as the officer of the day. (BL)

Right: Light artillery units were given a cap with scarlet cords and horsetail plumes. These bandsmen of the Third Artillery at the Presidio of San Francisco, in about 1866, have adopted the standard horse artillery dress uniform for their parade outfit, with the exception of the bandmaster (standing to the left front) who has a bearskin and specially made non-regulation chevrons, and the officer in his frock coat looking over his shoulder who is probably the regimental adjutant and is wearing his company grade uniform. (BL)

Left: The distinctive garb for hospital stewards evolved between 1857 and 1861. In the latter year the basic outfit finally was set as a single-breasted nine-button frock coat with crimson piping around the collar and at each cuff. A green half chevron with yellow borders and a yellow silk thread embroidered caduceus was placed in the center of the device and these were worn at downward angles above the elbow. By 1861, sky-blue trousers with a worsted 1½ inch crimson stripe was sewn down the seams of the trousers. A red worsted sash wrapped twice around the waist and tied at the left (as was prescribed for non-commissioned officers from first sergeant or orderly sergeant and above) where a model 1840 NCO's sword was suspended by either an over the shoulder belt or, after 1868, by a belt frog as seen here. This individual wears a jaunty privately purchased forage cap whose crown is lower than that issued to enlisted personnel. He also has an officer's small-style embroidered gold wreath with silver script 'U.S.' instead of the larger metallic insignia called for by regulations. White gloves complete the kit. This photograph was taken in the late 1860s or early 1870s. (FLNHS)

Below: The 1858-pattern black hat was not popular. Sometimes troops in the West substituted the forage cap even for parade as seen here for men of Company C, Third U.S. Infantry at Fort Larned, Kansas, in 1867. Otherwise, the brass shoulder-scales, frock coat, and other items are the regulation parade kit. (KSHS)

Left: William Zahn of Company G of the Seventeenth Infantry was photographed at Fort Yates, North Dakota, in the uniform of an infantry private as authorized from 1868 through 1872. In the former year the hat was to be looped on the right side for all soldiers unlike the earlier practice when only mounted troops wore their hat brims upturned on this side. The hat seems to be a private purchase rather than the issue item which was taller. (State Historical Society of North Dakota)

Below: The four-button sack coat began to be issued as a practical work and combat garment beginning in 1859. It soon became popular and was manufactured in large quantities during the Civil War for wear by the Union Army. Here artillerymen at one of the fortifications in San Francisco Bay go about their gun drill in the sack coat and forage cap that became so associated with the federal land forces through the early 1870s. Sheet brass cannon and regimental numerals ('3' for the Third Artillery) can be seen atop some of the crowns of the caps. Although regulations did not prescribe these insignia, which were manufactured for the fur felt hat, it was not uncommon for soldiers to add them to the crown rather than affix the company letter to the front which was prescribed by general orders of the period 1861 to 1873. This picture dates from about 1866. (BL)

Above: Captain George Wallace Graham of the Tenth Cavalry adopted a non-regulation black velvet roll collar on what probably is a waist-length jacket for field wear, although his high white starched dress collar is not in keeping with campaigning. Graham's low-crowned forage cap has gold embroidered crossed sabers with a silver embroidered '10' to designate his regiment; his shoulder-straps with their yellow background displaying gold oak leaves indicate his branch of service and his brevet rank of major which he received on 17 September 1868. (FAM)

Above: In this 1869 picture from Fort Leavenworth, Kansas, a sergeant (leaning against a field piece) is wearing the 1859 four-button sack coat. Chevrons with three stripes to indicate rank appear above the elbow, points down. These are of worsted wool and were sky-blue for infantry, yellow for cavalry, and scarlet for artillery. The leg stripe appears to be the 1½-inch worsted type required for all sergeants through 1872. The color conformed to that of the chevrons except for the infantry which had dark blue leg stripes. This NCO has a privately purchased hat but has chosen to draw the regulation worsted hat cord, an accessory which was available for issue, although the troops themselves commonly discarded the item. (FAM)

Below: Infantry officers at Fort Bridger in today's Wyoming demonstrate the diversity that existed in uniforms worn in the West from 1866 through 1872. All but one of the standing officers are lieutenants and captains which is indicated by their single-breasted nine-button frock coats.

The tall man in the 1858 hat is a field grade officer (major through colonel) because of the fact that he has a double-breasted frock coat with seven infantry officers' buttons in each row. The three military men on the far left are wearing shoulder-straps which were authorized for marches, fatigues, campaigns, and similar duties; the rest of the party wear epaulets. An embroidered bugle device is evident on the man with the bicycle as is the ⅛-inch dark blue welt on his sky-blue trousers which was regulation for all infantry officers regardless of rank. The two seated officers, who flank the white-bearded post sutler, are wearing civilian coats without an indication of their rank. Except for their forage caps, it would be difficult to determine that they were in the army. The individual standing in front of the doorway is wearing his sash over the shoulder which was the sign for the officer of the day. (NARS)

Above: First Lieutenant Mason Carter of the Fifth Infantry was similar to other officers of the immediate post Civil War years in the West in that he chose to adapt a civilian coat and vest to military service by simply adding his shoulder-straps with blue centers and gold embroidered bars and borders to indicate his brevet rank as a captain of infantry, which he was granted for actions against Indians in Kansas in 1867. A decade later, Carter would see action against the Nez Perce at Bear Paw Mountain, and would be awarded the Medal of Honor for his gallantry during this fight. (FAM)

Below: In an effort to take advantage of a large stock of surplus single-breasted foot overcoats on hand from the Civil War, the Quartermaster General ordered an additional longer cap affixed to these sky-blue wool garments, thus adding a degree of warmth as well as creating a look similar to some civilian overcoats of the Victorian era. This expedient proved short-lived after its original 1871 conception although a general order in 1872 required its continued use until stocks were exhausted. (SI)

Below right: From the early 1860s through 1872 the regulation undershirt, drawers and shoes for enlisted men were of the patterns shown here. (SI)

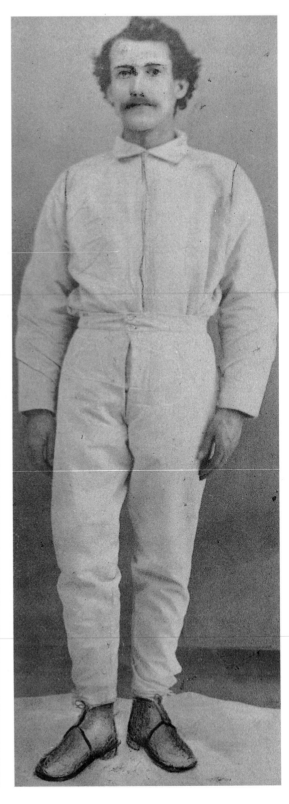

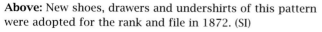

Above: New shoes, drawers and undershirts of this pattern were adopted for the rank and file in 1872. (SI)

Above right: This pattern of the long single-breasted white canvas stable-frock closed with three buttons. It was adopted as early as the 1850s. The garment was issued to mounted troops to keep their more expensive wool uniforms from being soiled. The canvas likewise could be washed easily, a necessary requirement because the color undoubtedly showed the dirt attendant with grooming of horses, cleaning stalls, and the other chores associated with maintaining a mount. (SI)

Right: Overalls of this pattern were worn under the stable-frock for cavalry and light artillery troops as of 1872. (SI)

Left: Second Lieutenant R. E. Thompson has obtained the new double-breasted dress coat with seven buttons in each row that was adopted in 1872 for company grade officers (second lieutenants through captains). The belt is of gold lace with four horizontal silk stripes in blue. The gold knots have blue centers with the regimental numeral in silver and rank devices of the same type as found on the shoulder-straps (plain for second lieutenants, a silver bar for first lieutenants, two silver bars for captains, a gold oak leaf for majors, silver oak leaf for lieutenant colonels, and a spread eagle for colonels. Trouser stripes were 1½-inches wide and in dark blue for infantry officers. (USAMHI)

Right: This side view of an infantry officer's dress cap is of the pattern adopted in 1872 and which remained in service for dress purposes until 1881. Flat gold cord trimmed the cap which had a gold embroidered hunting horn device on the front (replaced by crossed rifles in 1875) that bore the regimental numeral in silver in the center. White cocks' feathers rising five inches from the top of the cap were held in place by a gilt sheet brass ball and socket for infantry officers; scarlet feathers were assigned to heavy artillery officers who also had gold embroidered crossed cannon in lieu of the hunting horn. (NARS)

Right: Side view of the dress helmet adopted in 1872 for officers of light artillery and cavalry officers (in this case for the former group because of the crossed cannon device on the side buttons). The plume, which was scarlet for artillery and yellow for cavalry, and its socket have been removed from this *c.*1875 photograph. (NARS)

Left: Captain Gunther Sebastian, like many officers of his time, commanded a troop of cavalry while in his advanced years. Promotion was slow for most officers serving in the years after the Civil War. Sebastian is wearing the company grade uniform prescribed for dress purposes in 1872 including the top-heavy helmet with steep rear visor. The plume is yellow horsehair and the cords on the helmet and his chest are of metallic gold thread. The gilt eagle device on the front of the helmet bears a silver numeral '4' to indicate Sebastian's regiment, as do his shoulder-knots. The saber seems to be an enlisted man's model of the pattern adopted in the late 1850s. (KSH)

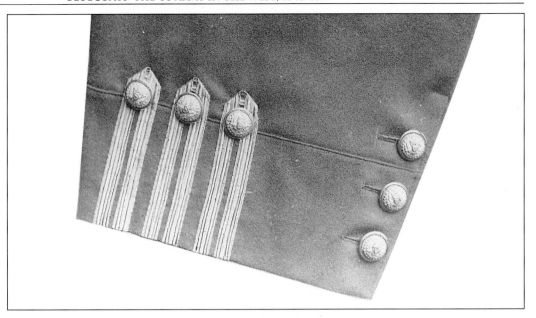

Above: Cuffs of the dress coat adopted for officers in 1872 had three gold lace ornaments for field grade officers whose double-breasted coats had nine buttons in each row. This example is that of a field grade officer of the staff because of the type of buttons which are shown. There were two gold braid stripes on company grade cuffs. (NARS)

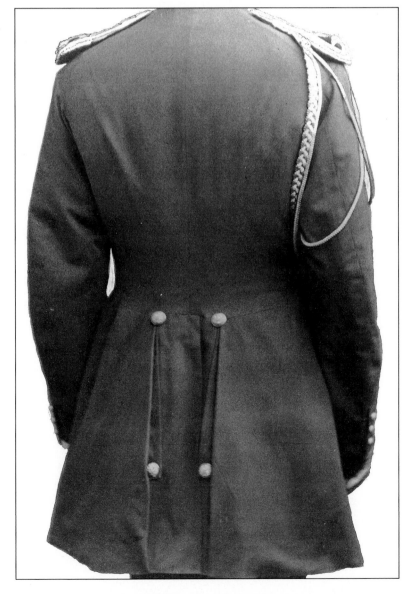

Right: The shoulder-knots adopted for dress purposes in 1872 also had a gold aiguillette attached to the right knot for aides-de-camp, adjutant general and inspector general officers, and regimental adjutants, as seen in this official photograph which also shows the back skirts of the 1872-pattern dress coat with the four buttons that ornamented the tails. (NARS)

Left: Captain Thomas McDougall of the Seventh Cavalry wears the dark blue wool dress cape with velvet collar over his 1872 dress uniform. This basic style of cape had been in use as early as the 1851 regulations. (LBNB)

Above: Officers from Fort Abraham Lincoln, including Lieutenant Colonel George Armstrong Custer (third from left front row), have all chosen to dispense with the rather ungainly dress helmet for this group photograph. Custer has ignored head-dress altogether, and the remainder of the officers tend towards the 1872-pattern forage cap with gold embroidered crossed sabers that featured the regimental numeral in silver embroidery above for cavalry, and the gold

hunting horn for infantry officers through 1875 (front row standing fourth from right, plus rear row seated second and fourth from left). The infantry officer in the back row likewise is wearing an old pattern single-breasted frock coat of the type that was discontinued by new uniform regulations in 1872, except for military store keepers who retained this style. Two other officers, Lieutenant Benjamin Hodgson (to Custer's left) and Captain Thomas McDougall, have procured non-regulation 'pillbox' caps, as has McDougall's wife. In turn, Captain George Yates (seated middle of front row) sports a fur winter hat and the model 1872 officers' saber. (LBNB)

Left: Unlike many officers of his regiment, this corporal of the Seventh Cavalry follows closely the 1872 through 1881 regulations for dress uniforms. The long front and back visors of his helmet are evident as are the regulation brass collar numerals which indicate his unit. Trim on the cuffs and shoulder-loops is of yellow facing material as is the 4-inch patch affixed to both sides of the collar. Yellow piping likewise ran around the top and bottom of the collar and down the front seams and along the skirt, which was split at the sides for mounted troops. The horsehair plume and one-piece worsted helmet cords are yellow to match the chevrons and the ½-inch leg stripes on the trousers, the latter two elements indicating the wearer's rank. (Bill Benthan Collection)

Above: Trumpeter Aloys Bohner of Company D, Seventh Cavalry, wears the 1872-pattern cavalry trumpeter's uniform with its distinctive yellow 'herringbone' trim on the chest that flanks each of the nine buttons of the coat. The gauntlets are privately purchased or a photographer's prop because these accessories were not issued to cavalrymen until 1884. Unlike many of his comrades, Bohner, who was born in Germany, did not die at the Little Bighorn. He remained in the regiment until his discharge in 1879, at which time he was the chief musician of the Seventh's band. (RBM)

Above: Charles Hendy (first row center) was the hospital steward at Fort McPherson, Nebraska, in 1873. He appears in the nine-button pleated blouse adopted the previous year for enlisted men as a general garrison, fatigue, and field garment. The buttons are of the type worn by staff officers, including surgeons. The collar, cuffs, and front yoke of the coat were to be piped in branch colors, in Hendy's case green for hospital stewards. He has the half-chevrons of green facing material with caduceus embroidered in yellow silk thread. The edges also were to be piped in yellow. The emerald-green leg stripes were to be 1¼-inches wide. Hendy is flanked by four cavalry privates in their 1872-pattern dress uniforms. (Union Pacific Museum)

Left: The collar, cuffs, and yoke piping on the 1872-pattern pleated blouse is more evident on this image of an infantry private (piping was sky-blue for infantry at this time) along with the new smaller sheet brass hunting horn device adopted in that same year for the dress cap and eventually authorized for the forage cap. The over-the-shoulder strap for the cartridge box was outmoded by this time and was depicted in error during this 1875 photography session for the quartermaster department. (SI)

Above: In 1872, an emerald-green trimmed Basque coat was prescribed for hospital stewards as full dress wear, with a cap that had matching green mohair trim around the top and base of the crown and on a vertical at the rear and each side. A green pompon, sheet brass eagle, and a gilt wreath with silver 'U.S.' also adorned the cap. Light blue wool trousers had green 1¼-inch stripes down the outer seams. It appears that this medical man has attached a civilian watch chain to the front of his coat. (FLNHS)

Above right: Post ordnance sergeants wore a dress uniform which resembled that of hospital stewards as of the 1872 regulation change except that their trim was crimson. A small brass flaming bomb device was affixed to each side of the collar. Crimson chevrons consisting of a five-pointed star surmounting three stripes worn points down indicated rank as did 1¼-inch leg stripes on the outer seams of the light blue trousers which remained the same as the 1861 pattern. A sheet brass flaming bomb device was attached to the front of the cap under the eagle while all trim and the pom-pom were crimson. Shoes were black leather. The belt was to have the rectangular brass plate with eagle and silver wreath, but the photographer's model in this 1875 image erroneously wears the 1839-pattern infantry belt and the over-the-shoulder cartridge box sling which also is incorrect. (SIO)

Above: A Medal of Honor recipient for heroism during an 1881 Apache attack in Arizona, Signal Private Will C. Barnes proudly poses in his 1872-pattern dress uniform with its distinctive orange trim on the coat and with orange cords and horsehair plume attached to the helmet. The model-1839 foot soldiers' belt is worn rather than the appropriate mounted saber belt. Perhaps this was a photographer's prop, or it may be that – signal personnel being often stationed away from military posts – Barnes was issued with a surplus infantry private's belt rather than a cavalry saber belt as would have been consistent with his mounted style uniform. The signal flags are red with a white center and white with a red center. They were worn on the left arm only by privates of the second class and on both arms by privates of the first class in the signal service. NCOs wore them above their orange chevrons. Very few of these dress uniforms may have been issued prior to the early 1880s. (NARS)

Above: After the rank of post commissary sergeants was authorized, General Orders No. 38, 20 March 1873, called for a dress uniform much like post ordnance sergeants, except that all trim was cadet gray (until 1880 when white piping was to edge the collar, cuff flashes, tail flashes, shoulder-tabs, and the front edge as well as split of the skirt at the rear for all non-commissioned staff officers thereafter, i.e., hospital stewards and ordnance personnel). German silver devices were affixed to the collar with points up and a larger version of the insignia was worn on the dress cap as well as the forage cap. A gray crescent appeared above the gray chevrons which had three stripes worn points down. The crescent was changed to white facing material for chevrons from about 1880 and remained so through 1885. (SI)

Above: A musician (left) and a private (right) of the Fifth Infantry Regiment stationed at Fort Leavenworth, Kansas, are wearing the dress coat adopted by General Orders No. 92, 26 October 1872, with its light blue facing on the collar, cuffs, shoulder loops, trails, and matching piping down the front, at the split of the rear skirt, and around a pair of belt loops. Instead of wearing the new dress cap, they have chosen to don their 1872-pattern forage caps which bore the company letter (in this case an 1858-pattern brass 'K') on the front until General Orders No. 67, 25 June 1875, called for the badge of the corps and a small company letter to be worn with the forage cap for infantry, cavalry, artillery, and engineer troops. (FAM)

Left: Topped with a white pompon and adorned with the new 1875-pattern crossed rifles affixed to his cap, this infantry private appears in the parade uniform which remained regulation through 1881 when a new type of headgear was adopted for dress purposes to replace the cap. With the ushering in of the rifle insignia all infantry enlisted personnel were to have a small numeral to designate the regiment above the letter of the company, both in brass, per General Orders No. 96, 19 November 1875. Musicians were the exception in that they were to continue to wear the hunting horn with brass company letter only. Later, General Orders No. 21, 20 March 1876, laid down that the company letter was to be placed in the lower angle of the cap badge and the regimental numeral was to be positioned in the upper angle. The belt is part of an infantry brace system issued on a trial basis in the 1870s. (WSM)

Right: Five black mohair trefoils appeared at the end of the braid which trimmed the chest of officers' jackets of the 1872-pattern. The same material edged the collar and skirts of the coat and ornamented its back as well as the cuffs. Shoulder-straps, which for some unexplained reason are absent here, were to designate rank. The hat is a version of the 1872 pattern which was designed to be worn folded closed or open with a flat brim, depending on weather conditions. The saber is an officers' model adopted in the late 1850s. (USAMHI)

Below: Another experimental item, the trowel bayonet, may have been sensible for entrenching in the field but appears out of place for the parade ground as seen here with men of the Sixteenth Infantry Regiment, including the band, at Fort Riley, Kansas, in their 1872–1881 dress uniforms. (KSHS)

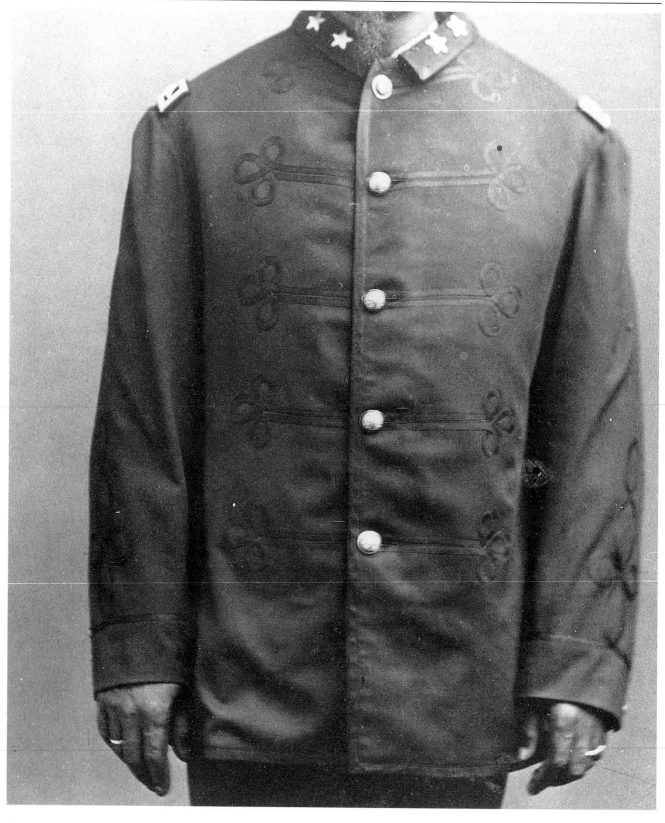

Above: This pattern sample of the 1872 officers' sack coat has a pair of stars attached to the collar. When the jacket was first proposed, brevet ranks (given in recognition of merit or valor, most often to Civil War veterans) were considered as an adornment for the collar, the individual's serving rank being indicated by shoulder-straps (in this case a colonel of staff). The concept of displaying brevet rank, however, was discarded before the blouse was adopted. (NARS)

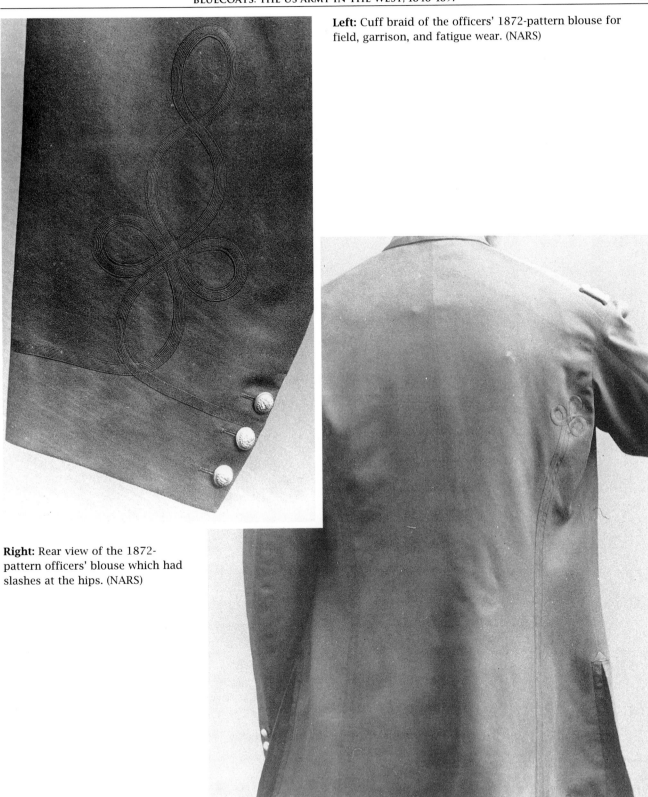

Left: Cuff braid of the officers' 1872-pattern blouse for field, garrison, and fatigue wear. (NARS)

Right: Rear view of the 1872-pattern officers' blouse which had slashes at the hips. (NARS)

Left: A couple of infantry privates wearing the 1872-pattern forage cap and the new 1874-pattern field blouse which had only five buttons rather than the previous pattern which had nine. The bothersome pleats of the earlier issue were discontinued, but the piping on the cuffs and collar (in this case sky-blue worsted cord) was retained.

Right: The official pattern sample of the five-button 1874-pattern enlisted blouse with cord on the collar and cuffs – yellow for cavalry, sky-blue for infantry, scarlet for artillery and engineers, crimson for ordnance personnel, emerald-green for hospital stewards, orange for signal personnel, and gray for commissary sergeants. (SI)

Left: An unidentified cavalry sergeant in the 1874-pattern blouse has chosen to wear a tie and vest, both of which were non-regulation and privately purchased by some soldiers for off-duty wear. Piping on the collar and chevrons are medium yellow for cavalry. (FAM)

Lower Left: The 1876-pattern campaign hat with its miniature fan devices known as 'Brachers' Patent Ventilators' had an overturned stitched-down edge around the outer brim. Sometimes 1858-pattern hat cords were worn with this head-dress although photographic evidence seems to indicate that the cords were not popular. (RBM)

Right: Theatrical in manner and dress, Lieutenant Colonel George Custer regularly put aside the wool blue uniform called for by army regulations and by the late 1860s was wearing instead buckskin trousers and jacket, with an appropriate civilian head-dress such as this fur cap for cold weather or a broad-brimmed light colored hat for field service in warmer seasons. He carries the 1873 officers' model Springfield. (RBM)

Left: Brigadier General George Crook opted for field garb that was practical, but not flamboyant. Here he has added a fur collar to a common enlisted overcoat of the pattern which served mounted troops from 1851 well into the 1870s. He has pushed up the crown of what appears to be an issue black fur felt 1876-pattern campaign hat in this portrait taken during that year. (USAMHI)

Lower left: Officers at Camp on Tongue River *c.*1877 display the variety of regulation and non-regulation wear that could be seen in the field during campaigns of this period. (FAM)

Right: General Orders No. 96, 19 November 1875, required that the hip slashes, and chest, back and cuff braid be eliminated from the officers' jacket, but some individuals opted to retain the mohair trim on the outside edge of the collar and around the edges of their jacket as seen here in the case of First Lieutenant Frank Edmunds of the First Infantry. The picture was taken in about 1880. Edmunds is wearing the marksmanship devices which began to be issued to qualified riflemen in the late 1870s. (FAM)

Left: NCOs from one of the companies of the Thirteenth Infantry, stationed in New Mexico, holding the new 1881-pattern helmet with distinctive spike, adopted for foot troops. Trouser stripes are dark blue and all trim on the dress coats is medium blue. (FDNHS)

Right: General Orders No. 102, 26 December 1883, sanctioned a cord cap strap, gold on silver, for the forage cap worn by all officers, as seen here in the case of a Fourth Cavalry officer. Prior to this date some individuals had purchased a similar or identical cap cord in lieu of the leather chin strap that previously had been regulation. (NARS)

Left: General Orders No. 45, 26 June 1883, called for an end to the colored piping on overshirts and enlisted men's blouses as indicated here by this sergeant who probably was a veteran of the Twenty-fourth or Twenty-fifth Infantry, two regiments whose ranks were filled by African Americans. He is wearing his marksmanship devices, and continues to exhibit his service chevrons, authorized for the dress coat from 1872 onward and for the blouse from 1882 until 1885, per General Orders No. 49 of that year. In this example, both the service stripes and rank chevrons are custom-made. (Herb Peck, Jr. Collection)

Right: Sergeant Charles Dunkinbrager has removed the numerals which designated his cavalry regiment from his dress coat collar and replaced them with a marksman device, a practice which began in 1884. Later, belt loops were no longer to be a feature of the dress coat according to Circular No. 9, 24 October 1885. (FAM)

Right: R. L. Sutton, a private of the signal service, appears in the five-button blouse which began to be issued without piping in 1883. He is wearing the German silver signal device adopted at least by 1881 for the forage cap as well as the dress helmet, and the red and white signal flags on his left arm only to indicate that he is a private of the second class. (Jerome Greene Collection)

Left: A cavalry sergeant with the reinforcing that was added to the trousers of mounted troops since early in the nineteenth century, is wearing the pattern of blouse with gray flannel lining that began to come into use in accordance with General Orders No. 32, 16 April 1884. The light-colored neck scarf is not regulation, but added by the sergeant for the photograph and perhaps for off-duty wear. Beside him can be seen a privately purchased straw hat which had been approved during the prior decade for troops serving in hot climates in lieu of the issue campaign hat. (FAM)

Left: The post quartermaster sergeant at the left displays the new chevrons and blouse prescribed in 1884; the seated post commissary sergeant is wearing the old 1874–83 blouse with piping (in this instance cadet gray) around the collar and cuffs and the chevrons with crescent worn points up until 1885. The infantry sergeant standing on the right is wearing the plain blue pullover shirt adopted in 1883, and appears to have bought a light-colored civilian hat which was preferable to some of the government issue campaign hats of the period. (Christian Barthlesmess Family Collection)

Right: A medium brown canvas suit which included one blouse with six India rubber buttons and matching trousers was issued with effect from General Orders No. 32, 16 April 1884, for 'each enlisted man of the Army who may be required to work on extra, daily, or fatigue duty ...' It was not to replace the white canvas stable uniform, however, for mounted troops. The previous year a practical, drab campaign hat with small wire screen vents on each side also became available for field and fatigue use, as seen here. (NARS)

Left: These field artillerymen at Fort Riley, Kansas, are wearing the duck canvas fatigue clothing with the 1889-pattern campaign hat that had a perforated snowflake on each side of the crown in lieu of the metal ventilator of the 1883-pattern. The soldier standing in the rear row middle has cut off the sleeves of an 1883-pattern dark blue wool shirt to make it a cooler garment while his comrade on the far right retains the shirt as issued together with standard kersey trousers and what appear to be 1886-pattern mounted boots.

Lower left: Brigadier General George Crook favored a civilian medium brown canvas hunting jacket and a civilian double-barrelled shotgun when he took the field in 1885 with his troops, including Apache scouts who are scarcely to be distinguished from the men they were pursuing. NARS

Right: The 1884-pattern officers' overcoat was designed to have a matching, detachable hood, although it seems that few individuals actually obtained this accessory. (NARS)

Left: From 1851 through the early twentieth century the lower sleeves of officers' overcoats displayed braid to indicate rank, with the exception of second lieutenants and chaplains. One black mohair galloon was the mark of a first lieutenant on up to five for a colonel and a special, more elaborate pattern (top left) for all general officers. (NARS)

Left: Civilians and officers mingle at Fort Bridger, Wyoming, five of whom are wearing the double-breasted Ulster overcoat of dark blue cloth lined with blue flannel which was closed by four frogs of black mohair and loops of matching cord. This smart looking outer garment was adopted by General Orders No. 117, 21 October 1884, replacing the surtout pattern of 1872 which was similar in general outline but closed with seven officers' buttons in each row. Both overcoats could be worn with or without a cape, or the cape could be worn alone as seen here in the instance of two officers who have chosen to wear them turned back to expose the inner linings which were faced with branch colors (sky-blue for infantry, yellow for cavalry, scarlet for artillery, orange for signal officers, and black for staff). All the military men are wearing officers' blouses of the 1875 pattern and forage caps. (WSM)

Above: The knots adopted in 1872 were to have a dark blue (frequently black in fact) background for staff officers which bore various devices such as an 'MD' in silver embroidery for doctors; acting assistant surgeons being distinguished by a silver bar on each side, assistant surgeons by two silver bars, and surgeons by a gold oak leaf to indicate their rank. (FAM)

Left: Resplendent in his dress uniform, this company grade infantry officer standing at attention has the white facings on his knots, gold lace dress belt with four white silk horizontal stripes, and white 1½-inch trouser stripes as adopted in 1884. He is wearing the 1880-pattern dress coat with seven buttons in each row for second lieutenants through captains and the 1881 helmet with spike for officers serving with foot troops (below the rank of major, with the exception of regimental adjutants who also were to wear the plumed helmet). (NARS)

Above: A post ordnance sergeant in the 1885-pattern dress uniform with its crimson facing trimmed in white wears the gold lace chevrons and service stripes (on the lower sleeves above the cuff) prescribed for all NCOs by General Orders No. 107, 12 September 1884. A spiked helmet with a small German silver flaming bomb device also formed part of the uniform. (Museum of the Non-Commissioned Officer, Fort Sam Houston, TX)

Right: Two dapper infantry privates in the pattern of coat laid down by General Orders No. 120, 24 October 1884, having white trim and the collar faced all the way around. The remainder of the army adopted the new collar the following year. The darker blue shade of trousers, as evident here, was first introduced in 1885. Stripes for infantry NCOs and musicians were to be of white webbing, until 1887, unlike all other branches which were of cloth facing material in branch colors. (Fort Sam Houston Museum, San Antonio, TX)

Indian Scouts U.S. Ar

Far left: Post commissary sergeants wore a nearly identical uniform to those of post ordnance sergeants except that the crescent appeared on the gold lace chevrons in lieu of the star (the crescents being points forward as of 1885), and the facing was gray piped in white on the coat. The crescent was also affixed to the shield of the plate of the 1881-pattern helmet which formed another important component of the dress uniform. (NARS)

Left: In 1884 Congress authorized post quartermaster sergeants to be part of the army's organization. Their dress uniform had been issued by the following year and featured gold embroidered cross key and quill motifs above the gold lace chevrons on the sleeves. The corps color was buff with white piping. The uniform remained regulation until a general order at the end of 1902 called for a new uniform. (NARS)

Above: Indian scouts tended to carry government-issue weapons and use a mixture of civilian and military accoutrements. In this instance the model 1876 cartridge belt and later Mills belts of the 1880s are slung around the waists of these Apaches serving in the Southwest, though little else of the regulation uniform is evident save the blouse of the first sergeant which is of the type prescribed in 1883 without piping on the collar or cuffs. Regular troops likewise often set aside issue items while on campaign. (NARS)

Left: Men of Troop E, Sixth Cavalry, at Fort Union in New Mexico Territory practise saber drill, although this weapon was long past its usefulness in campaigns against the American Indian. The photograph was taken c.1885; the guidon held by the fourth man from the left in the rear rank is the type that was regulation from 1863 through 1885. (FDNHS)

Centre left: In 1883 a drab campaign hat with a pair of small wire screen vents began to be issued and became popular with the troops, although black campaign hats continued in use with the proviso that the color was 'to be uniform in each troop, battery, or company', according to General Orders 113, 31 October 1885. As seen here, men of this troop from the Sixth Cavalry on the Mexican border in 1885 or 1886 have ignored this directive and wear both patterns of hat. (Arizona Historical Society, Tucson)

Bottom left: Sergeant Neil Erikson and two of his fellow troopers of the Sixth Cavalry in the 1885–6 Apache campaign depict some of the variants that could be seen in the field among these troops who took the trail in pursuit of Geronimo and others in the Southwest at that time. The corporal on the left has a Whitman saddle (the other two men have standard McClellan saddles) and is wearing 1876-pattern boots and the campaign hat of the 1876-pattern, as does Erikson who is in the centre. The corporal's shirt is of the 1883-pattern while Erikson and his comrade to the right are wearing 1881-pattern shirts with piping in the color of the branch (yellow for cavalry). All three of their horses have model 1863 bits, while experimental 1881 canvas saddle bags are evident in two cases as is a saddler's custom-made carbine boot at the rear of the trooper to the right who wears a civilian holster, as does Erikson who in addition carries a small non-government issue pistol. Erikson appears to be wearing 1884-pattern boots and issue gauntlets which were authorized in that same year. The saddle blankets are the gray pattern which began to be used in the late 1870s alongside blue versions. (National Park Service, Western Regional Office)

Below: Throughout most of the nineteenth century, regimental commanders were given great latitude in outfitting their bandsmen, but beginning with General Orders No. 104, 3 October 1885, bands generally were to wear the uniforms of their regiments with the addition of 'mounted helmets (having cords and hair plumes conforming in color to the arm of service, and lyres of white metal), aiguillettes with shoulder-knots [and small or large versions of] music pouches', as basic additions. This bandsman of the Twentieth Infantry essentially reflects the general order with the exception of the custom made white belt and the trouser stripes which appear to be either dark blue or red piped in white. (NARS)

Below: Although a German silver caduceus in a wreath was called for in 1881 as the insignia for forage caps worn by hospital stewards, this *c.*1885 image indicates that an individual medico has chosen to ignore the new regulation although he wears the type of five-button enlisted blouse of the mid-1880s with the correct green 1¼-inch leg stripes and the green diagonal chevron with caduceus motif which were called for at the time. (NARS)

Above: In 1879 enlisted men were to wear overcoats with a cape lined in their branch color, a practice which may have existed prior to the promulgation of a general order requiring this addition to what for all intents and purposes was the 1851-pattern light blue kersey greatcoat with its attached cape. By 1884 a pattern of overcoat with a detachable cape was adopted as seen here in the case of this young cavalryman who has removed the item for this portrait. (FAM)

Right: The 1885-pattern hospital steward's dress coat was modified slightly in 1887 in that gold lace chevrons were adopted in keeping with those prescribed previously for other NCOs. An arc of gold lace surmounted three gold lace stripes on an emerald-green background. A Geneva Cross in red facing material as an inset to a piece of cloth of the same material and shade as the coat completed the insignia. Acting hospital stewards did not have the arc on their chevrons and wore a small scarlet facing cloth Geneva Cross device sewn to both sides of their collar. Privates of the Hospital Corps had no chevrons but a white brassard with large Geneva Cross on the left sleeve. A German silver cross appeared on the helmet plate for all enlisted medical personnel. Trousers were to be of dark blue to match the coat, but this does not seem to have come into effect until the next decade. Stripes on the trousers were emerald-green with white piping as was the facing on the coat. The dress uniform for the Hospital Corps continued unchanged until 1897 when it ceased to be issued in lieu of a garrison and field uniform only. (NARS)

Above: According to General Orders No. 10, 4 February 1885, cavalry guidons changed to a silk swallow tail with the top half in red and a white lower half. The upper portion bore the regimental number in white and the lower portion exhibited a red troop letter, both in block style, and both centered on either side of the flag. These are men of Troop C, First Cavalry, in about 1890 because of the 1889-pattern campaign hats being worn. (USCM)

Below: Troopers of the Seventh Cavalry stand at parade rest during a formation held in 1890 or 1891, a period when that unit took the field in response to the Ghost Dance in South Dakota. They are wearing the standard field blouse of the period with what are probably 1876-pattern muskrat caps that had flaps which could be lowered to protect the face from extreme cold, and the muskrat gauntlets which were adopted in 1879. They also seem to be wearing Arctic over-shoes of the 1876 or 1889 pattern, which they are wearing over their 1888- or 1889-pattern leggings. (USCM)

Right: Several of the Apaches who enlisted in Company I, Tenth Infantry at Fort Huachuca in southern Arizona in 1892 seemed to presage Hollywood with their matching neckerchiefs. Such scarves were not regulation but purchased by individual soldiers to serve the many functions of a bandanna from practical use to accessories for the uniform. Despite the fact that these men are foot soldiers, two of them wear 1884-pattern mounted gauntlets. Three of them are armed with the .45-70 Springfield rifle, the workhorse of the infantry from the 1870s through the early 1890s, and which came to be nicknamed the 'trapdoor' because of its flip-up breech-loading block. (GAWHM)

Below: A darker hue of yellow was adopted for cavalry facings in 1887, as seen here on the dress coats worn by men of Troop L, First Cavalry at Fort Custer, Montana, in 1892. All enlisted men in the troop at that time were Crow Indians, many of whom had been scouts, as part of an experiment to incorporate American Indians into the ranks. The first sergeant on the far left, distinguishable by the diamond above his gold lace chevrons, went by the name of John Wallace. (NARS)

Below: Officers of the Eighth and Twelfth Infantry and the post surgeon (marked No. 11 and indicated by the 'US' device on his forage cap and the Maltese crosses on his collar) wear the short-lived 1892-pattern jacket with low standing collar which was covered in black mohair and bore the regimental numeral or branch insignia in metal on the collar. Five black mohair frogs and a mohair design on the lower sleeve as well as mohair trim around the edges of this dark blue blouse were similar in design to the old 1872-pattern blouse. Facings are white as per the 1884 change for infantry, although the officer marked No. 12 retains the old blue-lined cape. (USAMHI)

Below: Infantry Private Jacob Sherman, holding the .30-40 Krag rifle which began to be issued to infantrymen in 1892 with its special blue Mills belt to hold two rows of cartridges, an accoutrement prescribed for garrison, campaign, and dress wear as well. (WSM)

Below: Beginning in the 1870s with troops in Texas, white canvas clothing was allowed for use in the hot season. Not until late 1888, however, did specifications for a white cotton duck summer sack coat (similar to the dark blue wool five-button blouse) come about, as seen here for these Fort Brown, Texas, artillerymen at drill in 1893. They are all wearing the 1880-pattern summer helmet, including their officer on the right (behind the field piece) who is distinguished by his shoulder-straps. In actuality, there were no provisions for indicating rank on this uniform unlike its blue wool counterpart. (USASMHI)

Above, left and right: Blanket bags were adopted officially in 1887; the requirement to mark all such canvas equipment with branch insignia, regimental, company or battery level, and individual soldiers' identification numbers dated from 1882. This foot soldier of the Twentieth Infantry exhibits these markings on his gear. He is wearing the medium brown canvas leggings of the 1888-pattern with the 1889-pattern campaign hat. He is also carrying the model 1892 Krag rifle. (NARS)

Above: A member of Fort Riley's garrison wearing the new forage cap with sloping visor and round crown, which was called for in 1895. At this time branch insignia were adopted of one-piece construction having both the battery, troop, or company letter and regimental number (here '2 A' for Second Artillery, Battery A) cast as part of the whole. These were attached to the cap by means of a screw post. The 1888-pattern medium brown leggings are worn by this private while his 1881-pattern dress helmet and 1880-pattern summer helmet are on the shelf behind him with his canteen, haversack, model-1840 light artillery saber, and other accessories as well as personal items including a bicycle. (UKL)

Above right: The cape lining and chevrons of the enlisted man's infantry overcoat remained dark blue (in the latter instance piped in white) even after all other trim was changed to white in 1884 for this branch. Overcoat chevrons were worn below the elbow points down for all NCOs as of 1877. These too continued to be dark blue for infantry NCOs. Prior to that time chevrons were sewn above the elbow which meant that the cape often obscured the rank. The Twentieth Infantry sergeant shown here is wearing the 1886-pattern enlisted man's overcoat and 1895 forage cap. (NARS)

Below: Besides an 1895-pattern forage cap design for the entire U.S. Army, officers also received a different blouse design in that year which was a modification of the 1892-pattern. In the case of the 1895 pattern, the ornate sleeve trim was discontinued in favor of a simple mohair strip which ran horizontally around the cuff, a practice which remains today for the green service coat adopted by the U.S. Army in the 1950s. The trim on the chest also was discontinued. This second lieutenant of the Fourteenth Infantry wears the 1895 blouse and cap as well as the model 1860 staff and field sword with gold bullion sword

knot. All insignia on the blouse and cap are gold embroidery, although metallic versions were available, particularly for field wear. (NARS)

Below: The gold breast cord and pillbox hat with lyre worn by Chief Musician John F. Boyer of the Fifteenth Infantry band *c.* 1895 are examples of continued specialized accessories for bandsmen as are his officer-style knots. He seems to have additional gold piping on his coat collar. (Fort Huachuca Historical Museum)

Left: For dress wear light artillery officers, cavalry officers, field grade officers and adjutants of infantry all were to wear plumed helmets with scarlet, yellow, or white plumes respectively from 1881 through 1903. Boots formed part of the mounted dress as seen here in the case of this officer of the Third Cavalry of the period. (NARS)

Left: This light artillery corporal has his model 1840 saber suspended from the model 1874 saber belt. His chevrons are gold lace on scarlet facing material and his trouser stripes are of ½-inch scarlet facing material. His horse has the model 1892 bit attached to a model 1874 bridle. The canvas saddle cloth, which began to be used on occasion in lieu of the gray saddle blanket, is under his McClellan saddle. (NARS)

Above: This cavalry trooper of the early 1890s retains much of the horse equipage prescribed in 1874 with the exception of his model 1885 saddle bags. He is wearing 1884-pattern gauntlets and the model 1885 carbine sling. (NARS)

Above: The experimental summer helmet of the late 1870s began to be issued regularly by the next decade and into the 1890s, as seen here for men of Battery A, Second Artillery, at Fort Riley, Kansas in 1896. Chevrons and leg stripes are scarlet, the facing color for artillery. (UKL)

Below: This picture of the clothing department at Fort Grant, Arizona Territory, in the early 1890s indicates the rather sophisticated way in which uniforms and accessories were stored for issue to troops at a western post by this period. (NARS)